CLASSIC RECIPES

CLAUDIA MARTIN

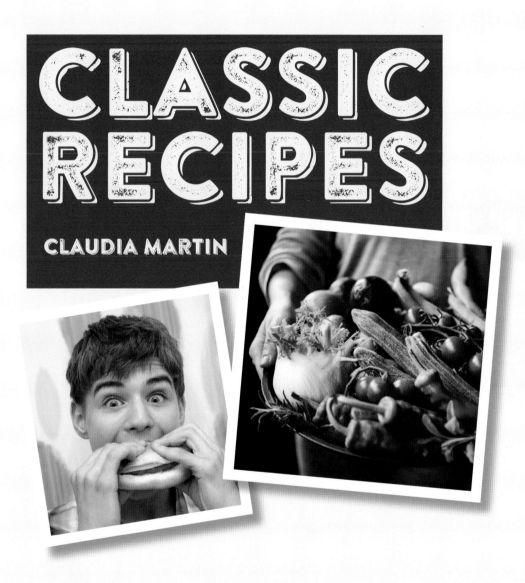

Enslow Publishing
101 W. 23rd Street
Suite 240
New York, NY 10011
USA
enslow.com

Published in 2019 by Enslow Publishing, LLC.
101 W. 23rd Street, Suite 240, New York, NY 10011

Editors: Sarah Eason and Jennifer Sanderson
Designers: Paul Myerscough and Simon Borrough
Picture Researcher: Claudia Martin

Cataloging-in-Publication Data
Names: Martin, Claudia.
Title: Classic recipes / Claudia Martin.
Description: New York : Enslow Publishing, 2019. | Series: Cooking skills | Includes
glossary and index.
Identifiers: ISBN 9781978506633 (pbk.) | ISBN 9781978506367 (library bound) |
ISBN 9781978506305 (ebook)
Subjects: LCSH: Cooking—Juvenile literature. | Cookbooks—Juvenile literature.
Classification: LCC TX652.5 M35 2019 | DDC 641.5—dc23

Printed in the United States of America

To Our Readers: We have done our best to make sure all website
addresses in this book were active and appropriate when we went to
press. However, the author and the publisher have no control over and
assume no liability for the material available on those websites or on any
websites they may link to. Any comments or suggestions can be sent by
e-mail to customerservice@enslow.com.

Photo Credits: Cover: Shutterstock: Monkey Business Images: bc; nenetus:
br; siamionau pavel: tc; Syda Productions: bl. Inside: Shutterstock: Africa
Studio: pp.32–33, 44–45; AngleStudio: pp.28–29; Anna Hoychuk: pp.38–39;
Blend Images: pp.10–11; Boyloso: p.28c; Buddit Nidsomkul: p.23; Cecop
aLp: p.30b; Chuah Chiew See: p.28b; Daniel Heighton: p.11; Daniel M Ernst:
p.19b; Dragon Images: p.46; Efired: p.44r; Elena Elisseeva: p.19c; ESstock:
p.5t; Garry0305: pp.1l, 16; hurricanehank: pp.18–19; Iakov Filimonov: pp.8–9,
12; iordani: p.24bc; ivan_kislitsin: p.38ct; Janet Moore: pp.30–31; Joe Gough:
p.27c; JP Wallet: pp.16–17; Konstantin Kopachinsky: p.10; LADO: pp.6–7;
lenetstan: p.32; Lentilka: p.37; Lesya Dolyuk: pp.41, 43t; Looker_Studio:
p.33l; Lucertolone: p.38b; MaraZe: p.44l; marekuliasz: p.27t; MariaKovaleva:
pp.36–37; Martin Rettenberger: pp.26–27; Michelle Lee Photography: p.33r;
mimagephotography: pp.40–41; Monkey Business Images: p.20b; Nejron Photo:
pp.34–35; nenetus: pp.6–7; NoirChocolate: p.17; Nungning20: p.35; Olga
Bondarenko: p.36b; Photographee.eu: pp.22–23; Piccia Neri: pp.2–3, 45, 46–
47, 48; Prasit Rodphan: p.15b; Radu Bercan: p.21; Rawpixel.com: p.27b; Rich
Koele: p.15t; RoJo Images: pp.14–15; Samuel Borges Photography: p.14; Sea
Wave: pp.36c, 38t; sergign: p.24bl; siamionau pavel: pp.12–13; S. M. Beagle:
p.43b; Somkiat Insawa: pp.42–43; Stock Design: p.19t; Sunlike: p.31; Svetlana
Verbitckaia: pp.24–25; Syda Productions: pp.4–5, 9, 13c, 20cl, 38cb, 42; Tatiana
Volgutova: pp.20–21; Timolina: p.34; Vankad: p.13t; wavebreakmedia: p.30t;
Yulia Grigoryeva: pp.1r, 5b.

CONTENTS

Chapter 1 Get Cooking!   **4**
Read the Recipe…   6
…Or Go Your Own Way   8

Chapter 2 Breakfast   **10**
Cheese Omelet   12
Breakfast Burrito   14

Chapter 3 Barbecuing   **16**
Hamburgers   18
Chicken Drumsticks   20

Chapter 4 Tasty Bites   **22**
Cod Fish Cakes   24
Meatballs   26

Chapter 5 Oven Bakes   **28**
Corn Bread   30
Turkey Meat Loaf   32

Chapter 6 Sides   **34**
Potato Salad   36
Crunchy Slaw   38

Chapter 7 Desserts   **40**
Key Lime Pie   42
Lemon Cheesecake   44

Glossary   **46**
Further Reading   **47**
Index   **48**

CHAPTER 1
GET COOKING!

Classic recipes are the dishes that most people have heard of. Everyone wants to eat them again and again because they taste so good! There is no better place to start your cooking journey than with the classics.

Why Cook Classics?

The classic recipes chosen for this book are commonly named among the most popular dishes in the United States. They were also picked to represent our broad and exciting cooking heritage, from Mexican burritos to Native American corn bread. One of the best things about cooking the classics is that they often involve classic skills, like panfrying or whisking. This makes them a perfect way for teenage chefs to build a repertoire of both dishes and skills.

Naughty but Nice

Are the classics healthy? Not all of them! Some of them—such as key lime pie and meatballs—are quite unhealthy because they contain a lot of animal fat, which is high in saturated fat, the "bad" fat that can lead to heart disease. When cooking the classics, it is best to think about nutrition so you can keep everyone healthy—and not hungry again an hour later.

Have a Plan

Every day, the following food groups should make an appearance on your plate: plenty of vegetables and fruits; low-fat protein, such as lean meat, fish, nuts, or beans; low-fat dairy produce, such as milk, cheese, or yogurt; and whole grains, such as brown rice or whole wheat bread. Whole grains have not been processed to remove the fiber- and nutrient-rich germ (kernel) and bran (outer layer). The carbohydrates from whole grains are absorbed more slowly into your bloodstream, keeping your energy levels stable. If you are cooking a meal for friends, though, you can ease up a little on these rules, because everyone can enjoy a double helping of key lime pie once in a while!

Store It Up

As you look through the recipes in this book, you might notice that some ingredients are mentioned again and again. If you keep these staple ingredients in your pantry or refrigerator, you will be able to rustle up a classic meal in minutes:

- Whole grains
- Potatoes
- Onions
- Garlic
- Lemons
- Eggs
- All-purpose whole wheat flour
- Dried spices and herbs
- Vegetable oil

READ THE RECIPE...

Ready to get going? The first step is to pick a recipe that will have your friends asking for more.

Take Your Pick

When choosing a recipe, think about who you are feeding—just yourself, a crowd of friends, or your grandma? Also consider the time of day and season. If you are serving brunch, turn to Chapter 2. If it will be a summer lunch, flip to Chapter 3 for barbecue recipes, or Chapter 4 for tasty bites to share. If your grandma is coming for dinner, she might appreciate one of the oven-baked recipes in Chapter 5. Anyone will love the sides in Chapter 6. If you are hungry for a classic treat, turn to the desserts in Chapter 7.

Go Shopping

When you have decided what to cook, check the ingredients list and equipment you need. Each recipe serves four people, so multiply or divide depending on how many people you are feeding. Make a list of the ingredients you do not have in stock, then take a trip to the store. Remember that some ingredients will keep for months or even years, while others need to be bought home no longer than a day or two before use (like meat, fish, and fresh herbs).

Hit the Kitchen

Always overestimate how long it will take to complete a recipe, so you are not still heating the oven when your friends want their corn bread. Read the instructions before cracking the eggs. The ingredients are listed in the order they are used, which should help you not to forget anything. If you are nervous about your cooking skills, take a look at the "Mastering the Basics" sections at the start of each chapter.

How Much, How Hot?

In these recipes, measurements are given in ounces (oz), followed by grams (g), as well as cups, followed by milliliters (ml) or liters (l). There are 240 ml in each cup. Sometimes, you will be told to add a teaspoon (tsp) or tablespoon (tbsp) of an ingredient. There are 5 ml in a teaspoon and 15 ml in a tablespoon. When a "handful" or a "pinch" is suggested, the exact quantity is less important—add more or less for a stronger or weaker taste.

Oven temperatures are given in degrees Fahrenheit (°F), followed by degrees Celsius (°C). If you are not sure how hot to have the stove, start low then adjust upward—it is better to cook more slowly than to burn!

...OR GO YOUR OWN WAY

The best ingredient in these recipes might be a sprinkling of your imagination!

The First Time

The first time you cook one of the recipes, you might want to follow the instructions closely and measure the ingredients exactly. Then, as you and your friends sit down to eat, ask yourself what you like about the flavors, textures, and colors—and what you could improve on. Is the cheesecake too lemony? Would you prefer a Tex-Mex marinade to a Chinese-style one?

Cook Like a Chef

The "Chef's Tip" box beside each recipe offers ideas for adding different spices or flavorings. Also take a look at the "Switch It Up" boxes at the beginning of each chapter, which offer even more ideas for ingredient changes and combinations.

Special Diets

If you have invited vegetarian friends for a meal, or you are vegetarian yourself, many of the recipes can be made meat- and fish-free—even the hamburgers! Check the "Switch It Up" sections for vegetarian substitutions. To make the recipes vegan, you will need to remove—or add vegan alternatives for—honey, eggs, cheese, and other dairy products.

Be sure to ask your friends if they have any other special dietary needs, such as not eating pork as part of their religious beliefs, an egg or soy allergy, or a wheat intolerance. In the case of wheat intolerance, flours made from other grains, roots, and legumes are often labeled "gluten-free."

Keep It Clean

Hygiene is very important in any kitchen. Before you cook:

- Wash your hands with soap and warm water.
- Make sure all your work surfaces and equipment are clean.
- If you have long hair, tie it back.
- Wash all produce under cold running water.
- When working with raw meat or fish, wash your hands after handling, and use a different cutting board and knife from the one for other ingredients.
- Never serve undercooked meat, fish, or eggs—make sure there is no pink meat, that fish is firm all the way through, and eggs are not runny.
- Check the use-by dates on all ingredients.
- Do not leave food out of the refrigerator for more than two hours.

CHAPTER 2
BREAKFAST

After you have tried these delicious recipes, the first meal of the day will become your favorite one!

A Healthy Breakfast

A healthy breakfast includes whole grains, low-fat dairy products, low-fat protein, and fruit or vegetables. Whole grains, found in whole wheat toast, oatmeal, and many cereals, will fuel your morning's activity. Dairy products (or fortified alternatives) such as milk, yogurt, and cheese offer calcium and vitamin D. Protein, found in eggs and beans, helps you grow. Fruit and vegetables—for example, in a glass of orange juice, tomatoes, or a handful of berries on your oatmeal—will provide fiber and many essential nutrients.

Our Recipes

You do not need this book to tell you how to pour low-fat milk on your whole grain cereal, so the recipes that follow were chosen for being classics that you will enjoy cooking and eating. Since they contain protein and vegetables, and can be served with whole grains, they are not the least healthy options out there, either.

huevos rancheros

Mastering the Basics:
Cooking Eggs

You can serve eggs in many different ways—as long as you make sure the yolk and white are cooked until no longer runny. Undercooked eggs are a major cause of food poisoning.

To fry eggs, heat a little oil in a frying pan and then cook cracked eggs over medium heat for around three minutes.

To scramble your eggs, whisk them with a little milk in a bowl. Then stir as you fry for three minutes.

To poach an egg, gently tip a cracked egg into simmering water, then cook for three to four minutes.

Here is how to boil eggs:

1 Always use eggs that are room temperature—a cold egg will crack when it hits boiling water.
2 Fill a large saucepan with enough water to cover your eggs. Heat the water until it boils, then reduce the heat so the water is simmering with small bubbles.
3 Lower the eggs into the water using a tablespoon.
4 For hard-boiled eggs, set a timer for seven minutes.
5 When ready, remove with a tablespoon and put under cold running water to prevent further cooking.

Switch It Up

The Breakfast Burrito on page 14 is a Mexican-style recipe. Want to cook other Mexican breakfast favorites? How about the classic huevos rancheros ("rancher's eggs")? You will need to fry an egg, then serve it on a lightly fried tortilla, topped with spicy tomato salsa. Another dish that uses fried tortillas is chilaquiles—top the tortilla with salsa, chicken, cheese, and refried beans.

CHEESE OMELET

This recipe makes four steaming cheesy omelets—or quarter the quantities to just treat yourself!

You Will Need
8 eggs
Salt and pepper
2 tbsp olive oil
2 oz (55 g) cheddar cheese, grated
2 scallions to garnish, chopped
4 medium tomatoes to garnish, sliced

Instructions

1 Crack the eggs into a mixing bowl, then beat with a whisk or fork. Season with a little salt and pepper.
2 You need to cook each of your omelets separately. For each, heat ½ tbsp oil in a small frying pan over a low heat.
3 Pour in a quarter of the egg mixture, then use a spatula to spread it evenly. Leave to cook for a minute or two.
4 When your omelet begins to firm but still has a little uncooked egg on top, sprinkle a quarter of the cheddar cheese over the omelet.
5 Your omelet is ready when its underside is golden. Use a spatula to slide under the edges of the omelet, then fold it in half.
6 Serve with a sprinkling of scallions and a side of fresh tomato.
7 Repeat three more times for the remaining omelets.

Colorful, tasty, and super simple!

CHEF'S TIP

Your omelets will continue cooking even when they are on the plates, so make sure you serve each one immediately.

BREAKFAST BURRITO

Invite your friends for brunch, then bowl them over with this tempting burrito!

You Will Need
1 tbsp canola oil
1 red bell pepper, seeded and chopped
8 eggs
Salt and pepper to season
1½ oz (40 g) cheese, grated
2 large tomatoes, chopped
4 whole wheat tortillas

Instructions

1 Heat ½ tbsp oil in a large frying pan, then add the bell pepper. Cook over a medium heat for eight minutes, or until the bell pepper is softened. Put the cooked pepper on a plate and set to one side.

2 Crack the eggs into a mixing bowl, season with salt and pepper, then beat with a fork or whisk. Stir in 1 oz (30 g) of cheese.

3 Heat ½ tbsp oil in the frying pan, then pour in the egg mixture. Stir to scramble the eggs as they cook, for about three minutes.

4 Stir the chopped tomatoes and cooked bell peppers into the scrambled eggs.

5 Place a quarter of the eggs and vegetables into each tortilla, sprinkle with the remaining cheese, then wrap up burrito-style and serve.

whole wheat tortillas

CHEF'S TIP
To add more of a punch,
sprinkle a small pinch
of chili flakes into your bell
peppers as you fry them.

It only takes a few minutes
to wrap up this recipe!

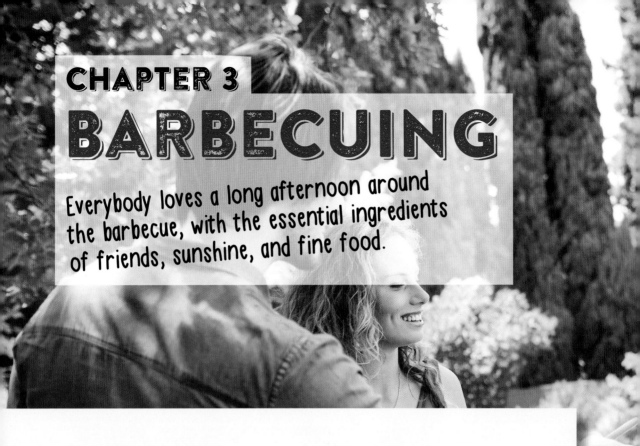

CHAPTER 3
BARBECUING

Everybody loves a long afternoon around the barbecue, with the essential ingredients of friends, sunshine, and fine food.

Planning a Barbecue

If you have never held your own barbecue before, follow this checklist to make sure you leave out nothing. Send out invitations and design your menu at least a week in advance. As well as meats and vegetarian alternatives (see "Switch It Up"), consider drinks, sides (see Chapter 6), and desserts (see Chapter 7). Make a list of the ingredients you need to buy, not forgetting coals for the barbecue. On the day, set up tables in the shade for food and guests, as well as a container for trash.

Golden Rule

If there are sides or desserts that can be prepared in advance, make them on the morning of the barbecue or the day before. Just remember the most important rule of barbecues: To avoid bacteria breeding, serve hot food immediately and keep cold food below 51°F (5°C). Do not leave food that you would ordinarily keep in the refrigerator sitting around in the sun.

spinach burger

Switch It Up

Not everyone eats meat. To make vegetarian burgers, follow the recipe on page 18 but switch out the beef and soy sauce for 5 oz (140 g) of finely chopped spinach, breadcrumbs crumbled from three slices of white bread, and 2.5 oz (70 g) of grated cheese. Shape into four burgers, coat with all-purpose flour, then fry in 1 tbsp of olive oil for five minutes on each side.

Mastering the Basics:
Barbecuing or Broiling Meat

Undercooked meat is a major cause of food poisoning, so never serve your friends undercooked burgers, chicken, or sausages. Knowing how to barbecue or broil meat properly is an essential skill. Here is how to do it:

1 Make sure your broiler or barbecue is hot, but not so hot that it will char the surface of meat before it is cooked through. A barbecue is hot enough when the coals are glowing red with a powdery gray surface. If your barbecue is slow to heat, cook meat indoors in the oven or broiler, then finish off outdoors to get that smoky barbecue flavor.

2 Turn meat regularly, and move it around on a barbecue or under the broiler, to ensure that it cooks evenly.

3 When you think your meat is done, remove it from the heat, and cut it open. It is safe to eat when no pink meat is visible inside the thickest part, it is steaming hot all the way through, and the juices run clear.

HAMBURGERS

These awesome burgers are perfect for summer barbecues, winter dinners, and everything in between.

No takeout can touch this!

pickles

You Will Need
14 oz (400 g) ground beef
1 medium onion, peeled and chopped
1 egg, beaten
1 garlic clove, peeled and crushed
1 tbsp soy sauce
4 burger buns
Ketchup
1 large tomato, sliced
4 lettuce leaves
1 large pickle, sliced
4 slices of cheese

Instructions
1 Put the beef, onion, egg, garlic, and soy sauce in a large bowl. Mix and squeeze together with your fingertips.
2 Divide the mixture into four, then press each portion into a round burger.
3 With the broiler on high heat or on a hot barbecue, cook the burgers for six minutes on each side or until there is no pink meat.
4 Cut the buns in half and spread with ketchup. Arrange the burgers, tomato, lettuce, pickles, and cheese in the order you prefer.

CHEF'S TIP
If you like your burgers spicy, swap the soy sauce for 1 tsp hot sauce.

CHICKEN DRUMSTICKS

Sticky and succulent, these classic drumsticks will be everyone's favorite.

Your guests will love these!

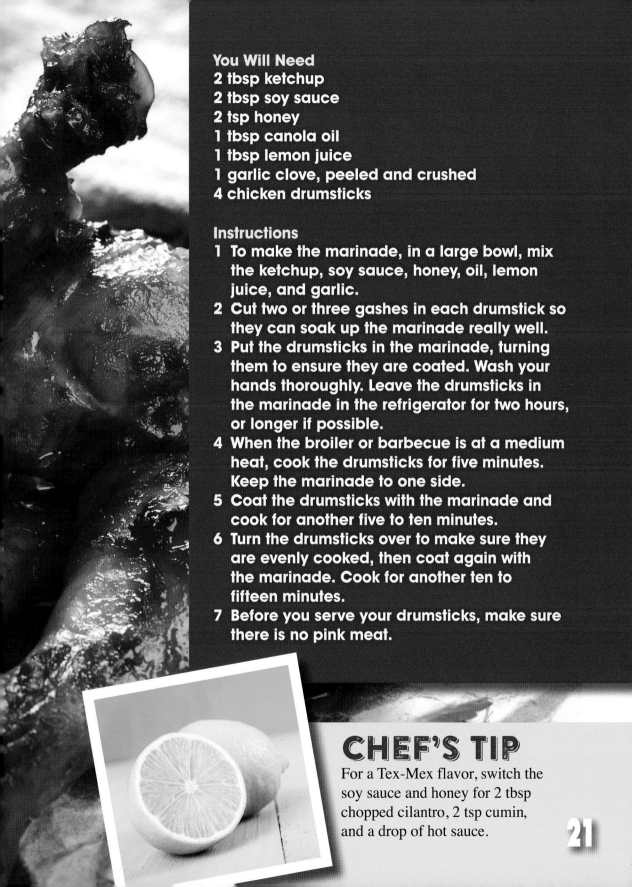

You Will Need
2 tbsp ketchup
2 tbsp soy sauce
2 tsp honey
1 tbsp canola oil
1 tbsp lemon juice
1 garlic clove, peeled and crushed
4 chicken drumsticks

Instructions
1. To make the marinade, in a large bowl, mix the ketchup, soy sauce, honey, oil, lemon juice, and garlic.
2. Cut two or three gashes in each drumstick so they can soak up the marinade really well.
3. Put the drumsticks in the marinade, turning them to ensure they are coated. Wash your hands thoroughly. Leave the drumsticks in the marinade in the refrigerator for two hours, or longer if possible.
4. When the broiler or barbecue is at a medium heat, cook the drumsticks for five minutes. Keep the marinade to one side.
5. Coat the drumsticks with the marinade and cook for another five to ten minutes.
6. Turn the drumsticks over to make sure they are evenly cooked, then coat again with the marinade. Cook for another ten to fifteen minutes.
7. Before you serve your drumsticks, make sure there is no pink meat.

CHEF'S TIP
For a Tex-Mex flavor, switch the soy sauce and honey for 2 tbsp chopped cilantro, 2 tsp cumin, and a drop of hot sauce.

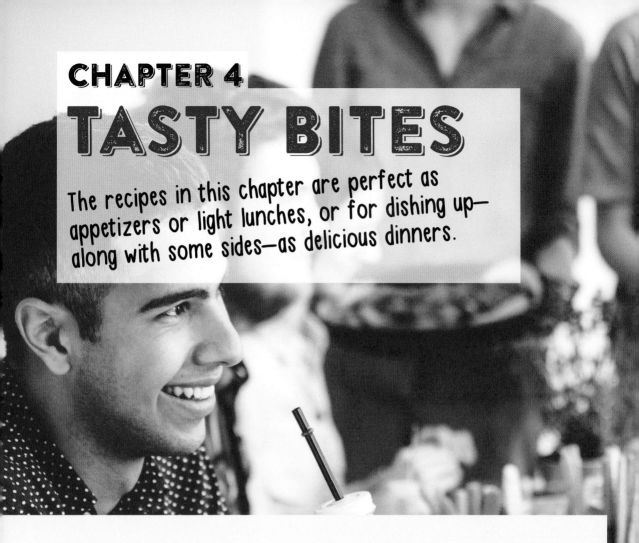

CHAPTER 4
TASTY BITES

The recipes in this chapter are perfect as appetizers or light lunches, or for dishing up—along with some sides—as delicious dinners.

Sources of Protein

Everyone needs protein to keep them healthy, so finding fun ways to dish it up is an important skill for any chef. Protein is found in meat, fish, lentils, beans, eggs, and dairy products. The recipes in this chapter—Cod Fish Cakes and Meatballs—are classics that appear regularly in kitchens not only in the United States, but also around the world.

For vegetarians, there are plenty of other options for tasty protein bites, such as the Middle Eastern classic, falafel. These fried balls are similar to the meatballs on page 26, but with a can of chickpeas and a little coriander and cumin switched for the meat and egg.

Mastering the Basics:
Frying

The meatballs on page 26 are fried. Frying to perfection is harder than it seems. Here are some guidelines:

1 Use a wide-bottomed frying pan or skillet so you do not overcrowd your food.

2 Heat the pan over a medium-high heat for two minutes, then add oil— 1 tbsp is usually enough—to keep your ingredients from sticking to the pan. Use a vegetable oil, such as canola or olive, which is low in saturated fat. Tilt the pan to spread the oil over the surface.

3 Let the oil heat for about one minute. Never leave your pan unattended because that is an easy way to start a fire!

4 Add your ingredients. If you are cooking whole pieces of meat or fish, meatballs, burgers, or unchopped vegetables, spread them evenly over the bottom of the pan, then leave to cook over a medium heat. Turn them halfway through the cooking time. This method is often called "panfrying." If you are cooking chopped vegetables or meat in a "stir-fry," that is what you do—stir every few moments, using a higher heat than if you were panfrying.

5 For both methods, watch your ingredients closely to spot when vegetables are softened and meat or fish is cooked through. For pointers on checking meat and fish, see the guidelines on page 17.

Switch It Up

When you have mastered the fish cakes on page 24, you could experiment with changes to the recipe. Try switching the cod for salmon or tuna. Alternatively, keep the cod and make spicy Thai-style fish cakes by switching the parsley for 2 tbsp chopped cilantro, 1 tsp grated fresh ginger root, 1 crushed garlic clove, and a pinch of dried chili flakes.

Thai fish cakes

COD FISH CAKES

Everyone should add a fragrant fish cake to their repertoire of go-to recipes!

mashed potatoes

Lightly browned on the outside and soft on the inside!

You Will Need
- 1½ tbsp butter
- 2 tbsp water
- 14 oz (400 g) cod or other white fish
- 2 medium potatoes, peeled and quartered
- 4 scallions, chopped
- 1 tbsp parsley, chopped
- 1 egg, beaten
- Salt and pepper
- 1½ oz (40 g) breadcrumbs
- Sprig of dill to garnish
- Lemon to garnish

Instructions
1 Preheat the oven to 390°F (200°C).
2 Place the fish on a large sheet of aluminum foil, along with ½ tbsp butter and the water. Wrap the foil around the fish, then place on a baking sheet and bake in the oven for fifteen minutes.
3 Put the potatoes in a large pan of water, bring to a boil, then boil gently for twenty minutes.
4 Using a fork, flake the cooked fish into a mixing bowl.
5 Drain the potatoes, then mash them with the rest of the butter. Add the mash to the fish, with the scallions, parsley, and 1 tbsp egg.
6 Shape the mixture into four fish cakes, at least 1 inch (2.5 cm) thick.
7 Dip each cake in the egg, then roll in the breadcrumbs to coat. Place the fish cakes on a baking sheet.
8 Bake the fish cakes in the oven for fifteen to twenty minutes, or until golden. Garnish with dill and lemon.

CHEF'S TIP
If your fish cakes do not hold together in step 6, try refrigerating them for half an hour to firm them up.

MEATBALLS

Serve these meatballs in a sandwich or with boiled potatoes, cooked red cabbage, and gravy!

You Will Need
3 tbsp olive oil
1 medium onion, peeled and finely chopped
1 garlic clove, peeled and crushed
18 oz (510 g) ground pork or beef
2 eggs, beaten
2 tbsp all-purpose flour
2 tbsp milk

Instructions
1 In a large frying pan, heat 1 tbsp oil.
   Fry the onion and garlic over a low
   heat for four minutes, or until softened.
   Leave to cool.
2 In a large mixing bowl, combine the cooled
   onion and garlic with the ground meat,
   eggs, flour, and milk. Stir and squeeze with
   your hands.
3 Press the mixture into twelve equal balls,
   then flatten them slightly so they will fry
   more easily.
4 Heat 2 tbsp oil in the frying pan, then add
   the meatballs. Fry them over a medium
   heat for six minutes.
5 Turn your meatballs using a spatula, then
   fry for another six minutes on the other side.
6 Check your meatballs are fully cooked
   by putting a fork into the center of one to
   check for pink meat.

flour

garlic

CHEF'S TIP

If your meatballs are oily after frying, drain them on a plate covered with paper towels.

27

CHAPTER 5

OVEN BAKES

Oven bakes are a great choice if you are entertaining friends because you can do all the preparation in advance, then relax as the oven does its work.

Old as Time

People have been using simple ovens to bake their food for more than thirty thousand years. From the start, baking was a way to cook proteins—such as meat wrapped in leaves to seal in moisture and flavor—as well as breads. In this chapter, you will find a recipe for the classic dish of meat loaf. Other meat dishes that bake in the oven include roast chicken and ribs.

Crazy About Bread

There are many traditional breads baked across the United States. As well as corn bread (see page 30), there are the Pueblo people's adobe bread; sourdough, brought here by European immigrants; New England's anadama, made from wheat flour, cornmeal, and molasses—and many more.

Mastering the Basics:
Using an Oven

Seems as easy as pie—and it will be when you have checked these guidelines:

1 Before turning on the oven, check that the shelves are positioned at the right heights, leaving room for your casserole or tray.

2 Turn on the oven when you start to prepare your ingredients, or ten minutes before you need it, so it has time to reach the right temperature.

3 Why do different recipes call for different temperatures? A low oven, at 250–300°F (120–150°C), is usually for easily burned bakes or for slow-roasting thick cuts of meat that would be chewy if cooked quickly. A medium oven, at around 350°F (180°C), is the standard temperature for many foods, such as vegetables, cakes, pies, and pasta bakes. A high oven, at 390–450°F (200–230°C), is used for quick-roasting thinner cuts of meat and fish.

4 Use only ovenproof cookware or baking sheets.

5 Rotate your food by ninety degrees during cooking so it heats evenly. If you have two trays on different shelves, swap them halfway through the cooking time—the top of the oven may be slightly hotter than the bottom.

6 As a general rule, the higher the temperature, the shorter the cooking time. For vegetables, a medium oven for thirty minutes should be fine. For a fillet of fish, a high oven for fifteen minutes is sufficient. Some cookies might need a low oven for forty-five minutes.

Switch It Up

The meat loaf on page 32 uses turkey, as it is lower in saturated fat than beef, lamb, or pork. If you really like the taste of traditional beef meat loaf, follow our recipe but swap the turkey for 14 oz (400 g) lean ground beef and 6 oz (170 g) chopped mushrooms. The mushrooms will add to the delicious "meaty" flavor.

CORN BREAD

Native Americans have made this delicious bread from ground corn for centuries.

Serve your bread with beans or chili.

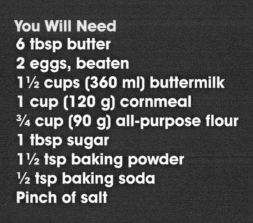

You Will Need
6 tbsp butter
2 eggs, beaten
1½ cups (360 ml) buttermilk
1 cup (120 g) cornmeal
¾ cup (90 g) all-purpose flour
1 tbsp sugar
1½ tsp baking powder
½ tsp baking soda
Pinch of salt

Instructions
1 Preheat the oven to 425°F (220°C).
2 In a saucepan, melt the butter over a low heat. When cooled a little, use 1 tsp melted butter to grease a roughly 8-inch (20 cm) wide baking dish.
3 In a large mixing bowl, whisk together the remaining melted butter, eggs, and buttermilk.
4 Pour in the cornmeal, flour, sugar, baking powder, baking soda, and salt. Stir in a folding motion using a large spoon.
5 Pour the batter into the baking dish.
6 Bake for twenty to twenty-five minutes, until the top is golden brown and a skewer or knife pressed into the center comes out clean.

cornmeal

CHEF'S TIP
If you do not have baking soda, use another ½ tsp of baking powder—your bread will rise just fine but may look less browned.

TURKEY MEAT LOAF

Meat loaf was brought to the United States by early immigrants from Germany and has remained a favorite ever since.

You Will Need
1 tbsp olive oil
1 large onion, peeled and chopped
1 garlic clove, peeled and crushed
20 oz (560 g) ground turkey
½ cup (60 g) breadcrumbs
1 egg, beaten
2 tbsp Worcestershire sauce
¾ cup (180 ml) ketchup
Salt and pepper

Instructions
1 Preheat the oven to 350°F (180°C).
2 Heat the olive oil in a frying pan, then gently cook the onion and garlic for five minutes until softened. Leave them to cool.
3 In a large bowl, mix together the turkey, breadcrumbs, egg, Worcestershire sauce, and ¼ cup (60 ml) ketchup with the onion and garlic. Season with salt and pepper.
4 Press the mixture into a baking pan measuring about 8 inches x 4 inches (20 x 10 cm).
5 Spread the remaining ketchup over the top of the loaf.
6 Bake in the oven for fifty to fifty-five minutes, then leave to cool for five minutes before serving.

ketchup

Worcestershire sauce

A plateful of comfort!

CHEF'S TIP
If your meat loaf cracks in
the oven, put a bowl of water
on the shelf beneath to create
steam and keep it moist.

CHAPTER 6
SIDES

The scrumptious sides in this chapter can be served with any of the savory recipes in the book. They are big crowd-pleasers so be sure to make plenty.

What's in a Side?

The nutritional purpose of a side dish is to fill the blanks left on your plate—need carbohydrates, add potatoes or a grain; need fiber and nutrients, add vegetables. Sides can be much more than that, because they add variety in flavor, texture, color, and aroma. If your main meal has no sauce, as with a fish cake or meat loaf, a side moistened with mayonnaise or vinaigrette can fit the bill.

Take Your Pick

The simplest side dishes are boiled or steamed. These could be potatoes, rice, or grains such as couscous; or vegetables such as carrots, green beans, or broccoli. Keep it varied by switching grains and the colors of your produce. A simple way to jazz up vegetables is to stir-fry them in a little sesame oil, with a pinch of chili flakes or a crushed clove of garlic.

Switch It Up

Raw vegetables are top of the heap when it comes to nutrients, so salads are a good way to go. Need some ideas? How about a classic Greek salad using chopped cucumber, red onion, tomatoes, feta cheese, and black olives, dressed with a splash of olive oil and a smaller drizzle of wine vinegar? Or take out the feta, then add lettuce, boiled egg, and anchovies—and you will have a salad nicoise.

Mastering the Basics
Mayonnaise

Both the recipes in this chapter use mayonnaise. You can buy mayonnaise or you can make your own. If you do make your own, shop around to find in-shell pasteurized eggs or pasteurized egg products. Raw eggs can contain salmonella, which is a cause of serious food poisoning and is particularly dangerous for children, the elderly, and pregnant women. Here is how to make 1 cup (240 ml) of mayonnaise:

1. Over a small bowl, separate one pasteurized egg yolk from its white. Do this by gently passing the egg from one palm to another, with your (very clean) fingers a little apart to let the white drip through.

2. In a mixing bowl, combine the egg yolk with 1 tbsp lemon juice, ½ tsp French mustard, and a pinch of salt, then whisk until frothy.

3. Splash by splash, add ¾ cup (180 ml) olive oil, whisking constantly.

POTATO SALAD

It is hard to think of an occasion when a potato salad will not go down well. This recipe serves four as a side dish.

Who knew a simple salad could be so delicious?

You Will Need
18 oz (500 g) new potatoes, scrubbed
2 shallots, finely chopped
1 oz (30 g) pickles, chopped
2 tbsp mayonnaise (to make your own, see page 35)
2 tbsp olive oil
1 tbsp wine vinegar
1 tbsp chives, chopped
Salt and pepper

Instructions
1 Put the potatoes in a large pan, covering them with lightly salted cold water. Bring to a boil, then simmer for ten to fifteen minutes, until the potatoes are just softened.
2 Drain the potatoes and leave to cool.
3 Cut the potatoes into bite-size chunks, then place in a large serving bowl. Add the shallots, chopped pickles, and mayonnaise, then stir.
4 In a container, make a vinaigrette by mixing the olive oil and vinegar. Now drizzle the vinaigrette over the salad.
5 Sprinkle with the chopped chives, season to taste, then serve.

capers

CHEF'S TIP
If you want an even tangier taste, stir through 1 tbsp of capers—these are the pickled buds of the caper bush.

CRUNCHY SLAW

This traditional side dish is the ultimate choice for any lunch or barbecue. Some traditions are worth keeping!

You Will Need
½ a white cabbage
2 large carrots
4 scallions
4 tbsp mayonnaise (to make your own, see page 35)
1 tbsp Dijon mustard
Black pepper to season

Instructions
1. Shred the cabbage using a grater or by slicing it into fine strips. Peel and grate the carrot, and roughly chop the scallions.
2. Stir your vegetables together in a large serving bowl.
3. In a bowl, use a fork to whisk together the mayonnaise and mustard to make a dressing.
4. Spoon the dressing over the salad, then mix it thoroughly.
5. Chill in the refrigerator for an hour or two.
6. Before serving, give your slaw a good grind of black pepper to season. Mix well.

Dijon mustard

A perfect mix of crunchy vegetables and mayo.

CHEF'S TIP
If you do not like scallions, leave them out, but add 1 tbsp of white wine vinegar for extra bite.

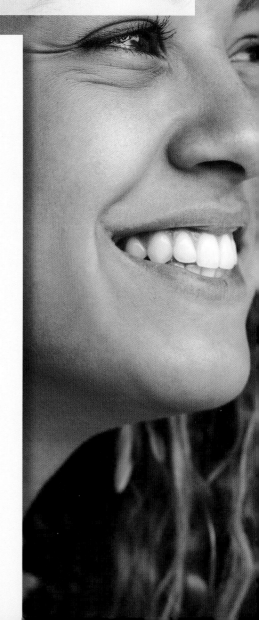

CHAPTER 7

DESSERTS

A tour of the classics would not be complete without recipes for sweet treats to finish off your meal, or to surprise friends when they visit.

What Desserts Are Classics?

A classic dessert has to be a dish so delicious that everyone wants to eat it over and over. Across the country, people come up with their own versions—a little sweeter, a little crunchier, with fruit on top. This is really true of cheesecake, one of the United States' most popular desserts. Chicago cheesecake (like our recipe) is made from cream cheese. New York style cheesecake includes heavy or sour cream.

A Guilty Pleasure?

Are the recipes in this chapter healthy? Not at all! There are options for making them healthier using low-fat dairy products (see page 43), or choosing dairy-free alternatives if you are vegan. However, as long as you eat healthily most of the time, a treat shared with friends and family once in a while is something to be enjoyed—really, really enjoyed—guilt-free.

Mastering the Basics
How to Whisk

Both these recipes call for whisking some of the ingredients. Whisking combines ingredients while introducing air to the mixture, so the result will be light and fluffy. If you have an electric whisk, it is a quick process, but start the whisk on a slow speed to guard against spattering and try not to over-whisk. Switch off the machine before putting a finger or spoon in to the bowl.

Before the invention of electric whisks, everyone whisked by hand and had the biceps to prove it. Here is how to do it:

1 Use a balloon whisk for whisking ingredients for baking. This is a teardrop shape with wire loops.
2 Pour your ingredients into a large, clean, and completely dry glass or ceramic bowl—not a plastic or wooden one, which could get scratched.
3 Tilt the bowl to one side. Loop the whisk around the bowl in a quick circular motion. This is the best method for introducing air.

banoffee pie

Switch It Up

The recipes in this chapter use a baked base made from crumbled graham crackers and butter. Once you have mastered making simple bases, you can build on them to create a range of other desserts— how about a British banoffee pie? Spread 13 oz (370 g) ready-made dulce de leche over the base, layer in four sliced bananas, then cover with 1 cup (240 ml) whipped heavy cream. Sprinkle with grated chocolate.

KEY LIME PIE

With the perfect mix of sweet and tangy, this pie will win the eternal gratitude of your friends and family.

Roll up your sleeves and grab a fork!

You Will Need
5 oz (140 g) unsalted butter
10 oz (285 g) graham crackers
4 limes
3 egg yolks (see page 35 for separating eggs)
1 14 oz (400 g) can sweetened condensed milk
1 cup (240 ml) heavy cream

Instructions
1 Preheat the oven to 320°F (160°C).
2 In a small saucepan, melt the butter over a low heat. Leave to cool.
3 Make crumbs from the graham crackers by pulsing them in a food processor or by putting them in a clean plastic bag and crushing them with a rolling pin.
4 Mix together the melted butter and graham cracker crumbs, then press into the bottom and up the sides of a roughly 9-inch (22 cm) loose-based baking pan.
5 Bake your base for ten minutes, then leave to cool. Do not turn off the oven.
6 Meanwhile, wash your limes. Collect their zest (outer peel) by lightly grating their skins. Cut them in half and squeeze them for their juice.
7 Using an electric whisk or a hand whisk, beat together the egg yolks, condensed milk, and lime juice and zest.
8 Pour the filling into the base, then bake for fifteen minutes.
9 Cool your pie to room temperature, then place in the refrigerator for at least two hours.
10 When you are ready to serve, carefully remove the pie from the baking pan. Whip the heavy cream, then spread over the top.

CHEF'S TIP
For a healthier version, use low-fat condensed milk or leave out the heavy cream.

graham crackers

43

LEMON CHEESECAKE

Everyone loves cheesecake, so how about making your own in under an hour?

It looks fancy but is totally stress-free!

brown sugar

You Will Need
16 oz (450 g) cream cheese, at room temperature
2 oz (55 g) unsalted butter
4 oz (115 g) graham crackers
2 tbsp light brown sugar
½ lemon
½ cup (115 g) super-fine sugar
2 eggs

Instructions
1 Preheat the oven to 350°F (180°C).
2 Melt the butter in a saucepan, then leave to cool.
3 Make crumbs from the graham crackers by pulsing them in a food processor or by putting them in a plastic bag and crushing them with a rolling pin.
4 Mix together the melted butter, cracker crumbs, and brown sugar, then press into the bottom of a roughly 9-inch (22 cm) springform baking pan.
5 Bake the base for ten minutes, then leave to cool. Do not turn off the oven.
6 Collect the zest (outer peel) of the ½ lemon by lightly grating the skin. Squeeze it for its juice.
7 Beat together the cream cheese, super-fine sugar, and lemon juice and zest. (If you like, reserve a little zest for decoration.) Add the eggs, beating until the ingredients are combined.
8 Pour the mixture onto the base, then bake for forty minutes, until the center of the filling is almost set.
9 Cool to room temperature, carefully remove from the baking pan, then leave in the refrigerator for three hours until the filling is firm.

CHEF'S TIP
To turn this into a vanilla cheesecake, swap the lemon for 2 tsp of vanilla extract.

GLOSSARY

boil To cook in a liquid that is so hot, it releases large bubbles of gas.

broiling Cooking by applying dry heat to the surface of food, either from above or below.

carbohydrates Food molecules contained in starchy foods, such as pasta, grains, and potatoes, as well as sugars and fibers. Carbohydrates provide most of your energy.

clove One of the sections of a bulb of garlic.

couscous Tiny balls of durum wheat, a very hard variety of wheat.

fiber Long molecules that are contained in plants and help with digestion.

frying Cooking in hot oil or fat.

intolerance An inability to eat a food without having side effects.

marinade A mixture of spices and other ingredients in which food is soaked before cooking, to flavor or soften it.

mayonnaise A thick dressing made from egg yolks beaten with oil, vinegar or lemon juice, and seasoning.

nutrients Substances found in food that provide essential nourishment for health and growth.

nutrition Eating well-balanced food that meets the needs of the body.

panfrying Frying food on the stove using a pan and a small amount of oil or fat.

poach To cook by simmering in a liquid.

protein A substance found in lentils, beans, nuts, seeds, meat, fish, eggs, and dairy products that is essential for growth and health.

roast Cooked food in the heat of an oven.

saturated fat A type of "unhealthy" fat that is usually found in animal products such as meat and dairy.

simmering Bubbling gently but not hot enough to boil.

stir-fry A dish made by frying ingredients quickly while stirring in a pan over a high heat.

vinaigrette A salad dressing made from oil, vinegar, and seasoning.

whisking Stirring or beating ingredients using the quick movement of a wire utensil, with the goal of introducing air to the mixture.

whole grains Grains obtained from cereal crops, such as wheat, that have not had their germ (kernel) and bran (outer layer) removed.

FURTHER READING

Books

Bolte, Mari. *Awesome Recipes You Can Make and Share.* North Mankato, MN: Snap Books, 2015.

Federman, Carolyn. *New Favorites for New Cooks.* Berkeley, CA: Ten Speed Press, 2018.

Pollan, Michael. *The Omnivore's Dilemma (Young Readers Edition): The Secrets Behind What You Eat.* New York, NY: Dial Books, 2015.

Rajczak, Kristen. *Great Grain Recipes.* New York, NY: Gareth Stevens Publishing, 2015.

Websites

Cooking Tips and Resources
kidshealth.org/en/teens/whats-cooking.html
Discover more cooking tips here.

Food as Fuel
www.dkfindout.com/us/human-body/digestion/food-as-fuel/
Find out more about how your body uses food for energy.

Grill It Safe
www.fsis.usda.gov/wps/portal/fsis/topics/food-safety-education/teach-others/fsis-educational-campaigns/grill-it-safe/grill-it-safe
Download fact sheets about barbecuing and broiling safety.

Publisher's note to educators and parents: Our editors have carefully reviewed these websites to ensure that they are suitable for students. Many websites change frequently, however, and we cannot guarantee that a site's future contents will continue to meet our high standards of quality and educational value. Be advised that students should be closely supervised whenever they access the Internet.

INDEX

Chef's Tip 8, 13, 15, 21, 25, 27, 31, 33, 37, 39, 43, 45

dietary needs, special 9

food groups 5, 9, 10, 22, 23, 28, 34

food poisoning 11, 16, 17, 35

health 5, 10, 22, 40

ingredients
  baking powder 31
  baking soda 31
  bell pepper, red 14, 15
  breadcrumbs 17, 25, 32
  buns 19
  butter 25, 31, 41, 43, 45
  buttermilk 31
  cabbage 38
  canola oil 14, 21, 23
  capers 37
  carrots 38
  cheese 11, 12, 14, 17, 19
  chicken 11, 21
  chickpeas 22
  cornmeal 31
  cream cheese 45
  cream, heavy 43
  eggs 5, 12, 14, 19, 22, 25, 26, 31, 32, 35, 43, 45
  fish 7, 23, 25
  flour 5, 17, 26, 31
  garlic 5, 19, 21, 23, 26, 32, 34
  graham crackers 41, 43, 45
  grains, whole 5, 34
  ground beef 17, 19, 26, 29
  ground pork 26
  ground turkey 29
  herbs and spices 5, 7, 15, 19, 21, 22, 23, 25, 34, 37

honey 21
hot sauce 19, 21
ketchup 19, 21, 32
lemons 5, 21, 25, 35
lettuce 19
limes 43
mayonnaise 34, 37, 38
meat 7, 16, 22, 23
milk 26, 43
mushrooms 29
mustard 35, 38
olive oil 12, 17, 23, 26, 32, 35, 37
onions 5, 19, 26, 32
pepper 12, 14, 25, 32, 37, 38
pickles 19, 37
potatoes 5, 25, 34, 37
refried beans 11
rice 34
salsa 11
salt 12, 14, 25, 31, 32, 35, 37
scallions 12, 25, 38, 39
sesame oil 34
shallots 37
soy sauce 17, 19, 21
spinach 17
sugar 31, 45
tomatoes 12, 14, 19
tortillas 11, 14
vanilla extract 45
vegetable oil 5, 23
vinegar 37, 39
Worcestershire sauce 32

Mastering the Basics 7, 11, 17, 23, 29, 35, 41
measurements 7

nutrients 10, 34

recipes
  altering 8–9
  barbecue 6, 16–21, 38
    Chicken Drumsticks 20–21
    Hamburgers 17, 18–19
  breakfast 10–15

Breakfast Burrito 11, 14–15
    Cheese Omelet 12–13
desserts 5, 6, 16, 40–45
    banoffee pie 41
    Key Lime Pie 5, 42–43
    Lemon Cheesecake 44–45
    vanilla cheesecake 45
dinner 6, 22
lunch 6, 22, 38
oven bakes 6, 28–33
    Corn Bread 30–31
    Turkey Meat Loaf 28, 29, 32–33
sides 16, 34–39
    Crunchy Slaw 38–39
    Potato Salad 36–37
    salads 35
tasty bites 5, 22–27
    Cod Fish Cakes 22, 23, 24–25
    falafel 22
    Meatballs 5, 22, 23, 26–27
    Thai-style fish cakes 23

Switch It Up 8, 11, 17, 23, 29, 35, 41

vegan 9, 40
vegetarian 9, 16, 17, 22